AFFIRMATIONS
for Anxiety Blobs
(Like You & Me)

Nanea Hoffman

DEDICATION

For my husband, Bob, and my children, Matthew and Samantha,
who have been unwaveringly supportive in all my endeavors,
who have provided humor and perspective and long walks, and who are my
whole heart. I am deeply grateful to my partners at Sweatpants & Coffee,
Shandle Blaha, Emily Parker, Jessica Hancock, Barbara Doyle and Tony Delgado,
for keeping the ship afloat and for just generally being amazing humans.
I'm incredibly fortunate to have you in my corner.

INTRODUCTION

Back in 2015, when the Anxiety Blob first came into being as a strange, vaguely worried, potato-like doodle, I had no idea it would resonate with so many of my anxiety-ridden kindred. I only knew I was trying, in my clumsy way, to show people what my own anxiety looked like: a soft, blobby thing in a pointy and often alarming world.
I had been diagnosed with Generalized Anxiety Disorder (GAD) and depression, and was doing my best to find coping strategies: therapy, medicine, self-care—sometimes of the uncomfortable but necessary kind—and, of course, the amazing and compassionate community of Sweatpants & Coffee.

This book is a collection of ideas meant to help you navigate that pointy world from someone who has often felt intimidated by it. I am not an expert, only a fellow traveler, but perhaps you will find a bit of comfort and encouragement within these pages.

And I hope you remember that you are never, ever alone.

"None of us are getting out of here alive,
so please stop treating yourself like an afterthought.
Eat the delicious food.
Walk in the sunshine.
Jump in the ocean.
Say the truth you're carrying in your heart
like hidden treasure.
Be silly.
Be kind.
Be weird.
There's no time for anything else."

—Nanea Hoffman

You do not
have to grab
onto every thought
you have.

You can simply
observe and
let them pass.

Sometimes you may feel lost,
but the truth is you're just on
your way to someplace new.

And you're bringing along all the lessons you've picked up out of the dust like bits of shiny treasure.

It's alright to
be scared.
But don't forget:
You've always
been an explorer.

Whatever adventure
comes next,
you'll be ready.

You are not
meant to be
in constant motion.

You are also beautiful
when you are at rest.

Have compassion for
the person you were.
Be proud of who
you have become.

Being gentle with yourself and kind to others doesn't make you weak or complacent. It means you're willing to listen. It means you're able to change and grow. It means your heart is learning to be resilient and strong.

Be unapologetic in your happiness.
Allow yourself to be as bright
and full as the moon.

You never know—
you might be lighting the way
for someone else.

Allow for
the possibility
of greatness.

You don't need a positive
attitude every second, and
it's OK if your version of
productive means you got
out of bed and...well,
at least you got out of bed.
Because maybe right now
that's the best you can manage.

In hard and scary times,
that's an act of hope.
Honor your reality, but remember
that hope is in each breath.

It's OK if you need to
distract yourself from the reality
of your life from time to time.
This is an important coping skill.

Take your
pleasure
where you can.

As you go about
the serious business
of making your way
through your often
complicated life...

...don't forget to stop for treats.

You cannot control
everything in your orbit,
but your anxiety may
be telling you that's the
only way you will feel OK.
Try to focus on what is before you.

It will take effort, but small, manageable actions can shift you out of rigid thinking.

Yes, the world
is full of worry
and strife...

...but there is still so much
to love about it.

Be curious.
Be interested.
Be passionate.
Be vulnerable.

Be willing to follow your
path wherever it takes you.
What's meant for you
will find you there.

Make your plans as big as you like.
Weave them out of sunbeams
and half-remembered daydreams
and whispered wishes.

Imagining a new story for yourself
is the first step toward living it.

Allow yourself
to be regularly
startled...

...and humbled by beauty.

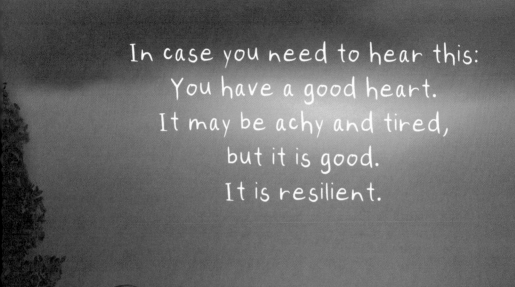

In case you need to hear this:
You have a good heart.
It may be achy and tired,
but it is good.
It is resilient.

Your heart holds so much,
so fiercely and
with such tenderness.
Don't forget that.

Your comfort zone is a clear space in the thicket of chaos. And that clear space is where we do the work. We catch our breath. We take inventory. And yes, we might also catch up on our reading and catch a few episodes of our favorite show. Mainly, though, it's our chance to be still, to let the swirling confusion settle so that we can see clearly again.

Remember that you can always return to this space. It's true that you're not meant to take up permanent residence in a cozy nest of solitude. You're meant to carry it with you.

We are all a bit
heartbroken by life,
but we are still capable of
hope and laughter.

Just a reminder in case you are in a dark patch right now.

Life doesn't
have to be perfect
to be beautiful...

...and neither do you.

Remember that you have
the capacity to surprise yourself
with what you are able to endure,
create, dream and learn.

You've no idea how far you'll go
or what marvels await.

Give yourself
permission
to be slow...

...in a world that's moving so fast.

Take time
to release
what no longer
serves you.

Declutter your life so the goodness
that is coming will have a place to rest.

Think of all the crazy, ridiculous, heartbreaking, difficult crap you've been through in your life.

The person in charge (you, FYI)
probably has a lot to answer for,
but mostly, congratulations are in
order because here you still are.
Keep at it.

You may not realize it, but every
time you share your story, you're taking
the hand of someone who thought
they were the only one.

Be the hand
you wish
you could hold.

Life becomes more peaceful
when you realize
you don't need to react
to every situation.

Conserve your energy.

How to get through when you feel
like you're not going to make it:
Just don't quit all the way.
You might have to quit for a little
bit, for now. Just until you can
breathe and find some space to
move. This is not giving up.
This is strategic self-care.
Realizing you can stop when you
want and start when you want
builds trust with yourself.

When you start to feel the pinch of despair, step back. Observe, like a kindly guide who has met someone who's gotten lost. Ask "What does this person need? How can I help them get where they're going?" Be patient and loving with yourself, do what you can and trust that change will happen.

There are wild places
inside you, full of
quiet and wonder...

...just waiting for you
to remember.

You're not here to
figure it all out.

You're here to love life and
allow it to love you back.

You can always, always find
a way to offer kindness to others.
Even if it seems like you have
nothing to share.

It's a better soul-boost
than just about anything.
You deserve to feel that kind of good.

There is nothing wrong
with having a great enthusiasm
for something other people
don't know or understand.

Your enjoyment is your own.

Even when you can't see them,
the stars are there.

Hope is like that, too.

Hey, remember that time when everything sucked and you thought your whole world was going to end...but then it didn't? Or when you thought the worst possible thing would happen—and then it did—but you still kept on living?

I just wanted to remind you of that.

Take the time to befriend yourself.

You are worth knowing.

Let go of
expectations and
make room for
what is.

Goodness doesn't care what you have pinned on your vision board. It just shows up and waits for you to notice.

Every day, you are becoming more and more the person you are meant to be. Be kind to that person. Give yourself good food, fresh air and plenty of light.

Be proud that you are embracing your life.
Taking responsibility for yourself today
is a gift to your future self.

When life feels too big, make your focus small. This next breath. This cup of coffee. This one thing your smart friend said.

Getting through this particular moment might be difficult, but it will pass. The next moment might also be difficult, but it'll be a different moment, and you can deal with that when it comes. You're doing great.

There is an indescribable
grace in allowing yourself
the room to mess up,
the time to rest and the
permission to continue.

Be willing to accept your missteps with the patience you'd give to a child who is learning to walk.

It's a profound thing to realize
that wherever you are and
whatever you are coping with,
you can always put up boundaries.
Maybe they are quilt-like,
stitched together from all
the lessons you've learned.

You can always make a place for yourself,
away from the noise and nonsense,
and fill it with meanings.

Don't be afraid to be
your weirdest self.

Your fun doesn't have to look like anyone else's fun.

It just has to
make sense to you.

Sometimes goodness arrives in
ordinary packaging. It sits there, ready
and waiting, in the middle of your busy
day until you happen to notice.

Be open to the sweetness of life.
Accept what is given.

Do what you can,
when you can,
with as much love and
honesty as you can.

And when you can't, rest.

Never underestimate
the power of the pause.

Seek out small moments of quiet.

Please remember that the thoughts
bouncing around in your brain
telling you you're not enough
are simply wrong.

Maybe those ideas
were installed there by people who
were lost in their own pain.

You can't do everything.
But here's the thing:
You're not supposed
to do everything.
Just focus on what's important
and do your best.
Whatever comes next
comes next.

Take a moment to gather yourself.
Just focus on what's most
important and do your best.
That's all any of us can do.

There is always a tiny bit of light,
no matter how lost you feel.
Stop where you are. Wait.
Gather that spark to yourself.

Hold it in your cupped hands
and let it light your way
as you take each shaky
step forward.
You will find your way.

In an increasingly chaotic and confusing world, it helps to remember that there are still soft blankets, and warm mugs, and kind friends, and good people...

...SO MANY really good-hearted people
who want the future to be better.
Take heart.

It's never selfish to take
a moment to center.

Find the still point where your secret heart lives and take strength from it.

Self-care can be as simple
as making plans with yourself
and then keeping them.

Make time for yourself.
Find out what brings you enjoyment
and feeds your spirit.
Take the time to fill your cup.

It's OK to be scared.
But remember:
You do things you never thought
you could do all the time.
You always have.

Do you know how amazing
that makes you?

YOU
ARE
MAGIC.

Saying "no"
can be
self-care.

Every time you say "no"
when you mean "no,"
what you are saying to yourself is this:
"I love you, and I will protect
your boundaries."

If you have the chance
to be kind, take it.
You never know who
might need it most.

Every act of compassion matters.

Perfect is boring.
You have a life that is comfortable,
and untidy, and worn in all the right places.

Life can be complicated and difficult,
just like you.
But it's also beautiful and worthwhile,
just like you.

You deserve the kind of joy that is wide and plentiful and full of peace.

You deserve the kind
of happiness that feels like
coming home to yourself.

Remember, it is a gift to
have your eyes opened.

Meet awakenings with gratitude.

You don't have to respond to negativity with negativity.
You don't have to pick up that burden.
You don't have to throw the next stone, cutting your fingers open on the sharp edges in the process.

You don't have to prove
you are strong by hitting back.
You can always choose to
stay in your own peace.
And who knows?
Others may decide to
join you there.

You can hold
yourself
accountable
and forgive
yourself, too.

Being unflinchingly honest
with yourself is
an act of love.

Be proud of
disrupting harmful patterns.
It takes a lot of energy and
willpower, but all that work
is worth the effort.

In case no one's mentioned it,
let me be the first to say:
You're doing a great job.

Growth is not graceful.
It's stretching, and breaking through,
and discomfort.
It's digging up roots, taking wrong turns
and failing spectacularly.

It's stitching yourself together into something new but somehow more you. Your hard work will pay off.

Within you, a piece of the child
you once were remains.
And that child somehow
managed to stay weird, inquisitive,
creative, loving and hopeful
despite everything.

How remarkable you are!

Do you know your purpose?
Are you acting with integrity?
Are you being kind?

Then don't worry about it.
Just stay on your path.

There are days, maybe weeks
and months, when you feel like you are
never going to move forward.
When you doubt yourself because you can't
see any tangible signs of growth.

But the truth is, if you're waking up every day and doing the hard, beautiful, necessary work of living and learning, you ARE making progress. It's impossible not to, so keep going.

Even the moon goes
dark for a time.

You are allowed
to wax and wane.

Feel your feelings.
All of them.

Just maybe don't make
big decisions while you're
still swimming in them.

Going through life hoping other people
will make you happy is like walking into
a fully stocked kitchen, never reaching
for food but hoping to be fed.

Reach.
It is your responsibility to
feed your own soul.

You are the one
who gets to say
what is true for you.

Your story is yours.
Believing yourself is an act of love.

You don't
have to be brave
every single minute.

Sometimes, you rest.
You say, "I'm not brave
enough for that...right now."
But you will be. Soon.

The best kind of gratitude is small and grubby and ordinary.
You have to squint at it and rub the dust off with your fingers.
It's the last stick of gum in the bottom of your bag. Or the crumpled five-dollar bill you find in your jeans pocket on laundry day.

It's the stranger who lets you pull
ahead of them even though you turned
your blinker on really late. It's the way
the air smells early in the morning.
That's everything.
That's grace.
Remember it.

The world is full of
exasperation and difficulty,
but try to love it anyway.

There are many different ways
to get where you're going.
Don't let your brain
tell you otherwise.

Choose the one that will
bring you the most happiness.

Please remember that every single day, you are doing your best. Every day, you're doing what you can with what you've got in the tank.

And every day,
you are moving a little farther along.
Enjoy the ride.

Dreams and hopes
are powerful.

They carry you toward your goals
if you hang on tight.

Every day,
you have small opportunities
to care for yourself.

Try to be present in those moments.

Allow yourself to exist in complexity.
You can be sorrowful and still laugh.
You can be tired and in pain but still be
moving and doing. You can have salad
for lunch and French fries for dinner.

You cannot be simplified into one neat, little bundle. You're a wondrous ball of contradiction and beauty.

Treat yourself as you would a beloved plant.

Air, light, water, nourishment and proper care are necessary for you to blossom and grow.

Every so often, take a step back from
the constant noise and distraction.

Breathe.

Observe the moment for what it is.

Look with compassionate eyes
at your life and
all the little lights in it.

Once in a while, as you're working your way through your list of Have Tos, take a look at your list of Want Tos. Not so you can drop everything and go chasing after them right that minute, which might not be practical, but as a reference point so you know what you're working toward.

Keep happiness in your focus.

Life can be scary and unpredictable,
but keep your eyes on the horizon
and remember...

...learning to find your balance
is also an adventure.

Be considerate to yourself.
Take yourself for walks and lunches.
Listen intently to what
your inner self is saying.

Discover how
extraordinary you are.

It's totally OK if you don't have a "calling" or some grand, impressive purpose. You're living a life. You're figuring it out, moment by moment.

You're waking up every day,
even when the waters
are choppy and bleak,
and you're looking for brighter skies.
That's such an admirable thing.

When you are having a
difficult time, remember
that there are still places
of beckoning warmth,
light and acceptance
calling to you.

You might not be able to
find them on a map,
but you'll know them
when you find them.
Look. Listen.
They'll guide you.

Some days, you may feel like you're not making progress at all, but treading water is a good skill to have.

Sometimes keeping
your head above water
can be enough.

It's not easy to be a tender thing in a world full of pointy and jagged edges. But look around you: soft things thrive everywhere. You can, too. Don't change your heart or let yourself go apathetic and dull.

Be wise. Be kind.
Retreat to safety when necessary,
but remember to come back and live
in the moment with your loved ones.
The world needs softness.
That is a form of strength.

There is a clear,
still space inside you.
Sometimes it's hard to find,
and you might temporarily forget
the way, but it's always there.

The more you visit,
the easier it is to return.

Some things don't heal.
You make peace with the pain.
Maybe it has something
to teach you.
Or maybe it's a price
you are willing to pay.

Or maybe you just love yourself through it and allow that to be enough.

No matter what,
no matter how painful or awkward
or weird the situation is, all you can
really do is come as yourself.

So, be the SELFIEST SELF you can be.
The most you.
The truest you. You will make it,
you magnificent human, you!

Make wishes.
Envision a life
that is satisfying
and full of possibility.

Cast your intentions into the world
with love and determination
and watch what happens.

Dare to imagine a future
for yourself
that is full and bright...

...and see how far you soar.

"Whole" does not have to mean:
* happy at any given moment
* conforming to ideals
of physical health
* free of mental health issues
* unscathed by trauma
* healed from trauma
* perpetually positive
* constantly grateful
*totally fulfilled

"Whole" means you LOVE yourself.
All of you, including the parts
other people told you were unlovable.
Maybe you're there, and maybe you're
crawling toward it like so many of us.
Either way, you're doing great.

You may get tired and frustrated, and you may lose your footing more times than you can count. But try to love yourself for your persistence.

Don't worry about wanting what
other people think you should want.

Peace in your heart
is an achievement.
Calm in your mind
is an achievement.
Kindness in your actions
is an achievement.
These are always worthy goals.

When you are authentically
aligned with your beliefs
and are true to yourself,
good things follow.

And some of those
things might be
out of this world.

There will be days when you will need to be alone, away from the busy world.

You may huddle under a blanket while
you quiet your brain and make a plan.
You are not defective; you are recharging.

Nourish yourself in all the important ways:
physically, mentally and emotionally.

When you take care of yourself,
you are making the world
a happier place.

Anxiety makes you time travel. You're always floating off into the scary, imaginary future or getting stuck in the shame-inducing past. Anywhere but right here, which is where you belong.

When you catch yourself at it—you won't always (and that's fine), but when you do—gently take hold of your balloon string and reel yourself home. You are here. Right now. You can get through this moment. Breathe, anchor, repeat.

Maybe it's not
the dream you hoped for.
That's OK.

There's a before and an after,
and both can be beautiful.

Take one moment
and be still now.
Feel the breath in your body
which has endured so much
and still holds you with love.

Look around at this complicated,
heartbreaking, still-beautiful world
and know that it is your home.
And you will always belong in it.

When you are feeling lonely
and sad and other,
it can seem as if you are utterly alone.
Your feelings are real
but they aren't always true.

Reach out. Let the safe people in your life know how you are feeling. You'll be glad you did. This moment is only a moment. It will pass. Promise.

Your heart doesn't
need to be fixed.
There's nothing wrong with it.

It just needs to be seen
and held and loved.

Of course you'll occasionally find
yourself in unfamiliar territory.
It's inevitable for travelers.
But remember:
You are home.
You are home.
You are home.

You are here.
You are not lost.
You belong.

It's quite easy to forget that life is more
than rushing from one task to the next,
or who thinks what about whatever,
or how much you've done or achieved.
Did you live today?
Did you experience gratitude,
even for just a moment?

Right now, someone else is reading this, just like you are, and you're connected, perhaps across a vast distance. That. Remember that.

There is a certain
kind of light that
only you can
put out into the
universe.
It's OK if you don't
totally understand
what it is,
what it looks like
or why.

Just know that
you are so very beautiful
as you try so earnestly
to be yourself in the world.

You don't always have to know what you're doing. You just have to remember who you are, what makes you happy and what you won't tolerate.

The rest will sort itself out.

Life is full of twists and drops and swooping curves you might never see coming. It might even turn you completely upside down.

It's exciting, and wonderful,
and terrifying, and tragic.
But it's so great that you're
here for the ride.

You deserve that.
Honor those efforts.

You are so beautiful
when you get lost in a thing
that truly matters
to you—how lit up and
serious and focused you are.

It's so very lovely.

Attend to your life in every sense.

Be present for it.
Show up every day
to the classroom that is your life.
Pay close attention.

You've reached the end,
but you are still beginning.
And of course,
it's never too late to start over.

MORE HELP FROM NANEA HOFFMAN!

A page-by-page remedy for the Anxiety Blob in all of us.

ABOUT THE AUTHOR

Nanea Hoffman is the founder of Sweatpants & Coffee, a social media platform, online community and lifestyle brand focused on comfort, creativity, inspiration and fun. She launched SweatpantsAndCoffee.com in 2013 as a place to explore the joys of everyday life and to foster meaningful connection. An avid builder of blanket forts since childhood, her goal has been to make Sweatpants & Coffee the coziest corner of the internet. She is also the creator of the Anxiety Blob, a physical representation of her own anxiety disorder, which has since become a beloved mental health mascot for people around the world. The Anxiety Blob is a reminder that you are not alone, and that you are more than your anxiety.

Want your own Anxiety Blob? Go to SweatpantsAndCoffee.com to find your newest friend!

ACKNOWLEDGEMENTS

Sweatpants & Coffee would not exist without my dear friends and amazing partners Jessica Hancock, Shandle Blaha, Emily Parker, Barbara Doyle and Tony Delgado. Thank you for putting up with me, providing much needed perspective and laughter, and for keeping the place running. You hold up this blanket fort. I am humbled by and grateful for the wonderful community of kindreds, writers and fans who believed in this dream and who helped to make it a reality. Last, but certainly not least, I thank my husband, Bob, who is the best person I know and who holds my hand every step of the way, and my children, Matthew and Samantha, who are my heart. "I love you every."

Media Lab Books
For inquiries, call 646-838-6637

Copyright 2021 Topix Media Lab

Published by Topix Media Lab
14 Wall Street, Suite 4B
New York, NY 10005

Printed in Korea

ISBN-13: 978-1-948174-84-8
ISBN-10: 1-948174-84-7

Nanea Hoffman
Founder/Editor-in-Chief
All illustrations Nanea Hoffman.

PA-H21-1